I0162238

MINIMALISM

23 Steps To Decluttering & Organizing Your Home

Keli Mable

**Creator of The Divide & Decide Method™
and the Refrain & Contain Method™**

CLADD
PUBLISHING

Copyright © 2017 by Cladd Publishing Inc.
All rights reserved.

Except as permitted under the United States Copyright act of 1976, no part of this publication may be reproduced or distributed in any form or by any means, or stored in a database or retrieval system, without prior written permission of the publisher.

Cladd Publishing Inc.
USA

This publication is designed to provide accurate information regarding the subject matter covered. It is sold with the understanding that neither the author nor the publisher is providing medical, legal or other professional advice or services. Always seek advice from a competent professional before using any of the information in this book. The author and the publisher specifically disclaim any liability that is incurred from the use or application of the contents of this book.

Minimalism: 23 Steps To Decluttering & Organizing Your Home

ISBN 978-1-946881-32-8 (e-book)
ISBN 978-1-946881-31-1 (paperback)

Contents

STEP 1: A JOURNEY WORTH TAKING 7

STEP 2: WHY PEOPLE CLUTTER.. 9

STEP 3: CLUTTER IS RUINING YOUR LIFE 13

STEP 4: DECLUTTERING BOOST YOUR HEALTH & VITALITY 19

STEP 5: DANGERS OF A MESSY DESK AT WORK 21

STEP 6: LIFE IS OUT OF CONTROL 23

STEP 7: CLUTTER = WASTED MONEY 25

STEP 8: STORAGE METHODS WILL NOT SOLVE PROBLEMS ALONE.........27

STEP 9: DIVIDE & DECIDE DECLUTTERING METHOD 29

STEP 10: ORGANIZE ENTIRE HOME BY CATEGORY – NOT BY ROOM 31

STEP 11: SETTING UP PRACTICAL ORGANIZATION & STORAGE 33

STEP 12: DECLUTTER/ORGANIZE/STORE ALL AT ONCE........................37

STEP 13: REFRAIN & CONTAIN 39

STEP 14: RAISE A CLUTTER FREE CHILD.....................................41

STEP 16: KITCHEN CLEANSE 47

STEP 15: JUNK-DRAWER PERFECTION IN 30 MINUTES 51

STEP 17: BATHROOM SOLUTIONS..57

STEP 18: TRANSFORM YOUR CLOSET 63

STEP 19: STORE YOUR BEAUTY PRODUCTS, BEAUTIFULLY! 65

STEP 20: ORGANIZING PET SUPPLIES 69

STEP 21: DECLUTTERING DIGITAL & PRINTED PICTURES 75

STEP 22: GARAGE OVERHAUL 79

STEP 23: GUIDE TO TACKLING THE SPICE CABINET 51

FINAL THOUGHTS 85

Step 1: A Journey Worth Taking

Living a simplified, uncluttered life with less useless junk, sounds attractive to many. You have probably considered the benefits of owning fewer possessions: less to clean, less debt, less to organize, less stress, more money and energy for the things that you really want.

Many begin to feel overwhelmed, anxious, and defeated around the idea of decluttering and organizing their entire home. The process doesn't need to be as painful as some make it out to be. In fact, the journey is one of the most rewarding things you will do for yourself and your family. When completed you will feel energized and ready to take on the world.

Step 2: Why People Clutter

A cluttered home makes us feel out of control. You might start blaming yourself for not having your act together. You could think something is wrong with you. Maybe you're just a messy person. Maybe you're lazy.

But what if you are just a normal person with a few legitimate reasons for the chaotic state of your home? Once you understand why the clutter occurs, the solutions become easier to solve than you think.

HERE ARE FOUR REASONS YOU MIGHT HAVE A CLUTTER PROBLEM:

1. **You Buy Too Much = Wasted Money**
   This might seem like the most obvious reason for clutter, but it is usually the one we have the most trouble with. We can't find that one special shirt because our closet is so packed. We run out and purchase new tools because our garage is packed to the brim, and we can't easily find our screwdriver. Too much stuff

always creates more clutter, leading to lost items that we waste more money replacing.

2. Changes = Piles of Useless Stuff

Every time we have a change in routine, we tend to change the items we regularly use. Whether we are going through a stressful period, holiday seasons, had a baby, lost or started a new job, financial setbacks, move to another home, had surgery, or have any other life-altering experience, piles of clutter multiply. We tend to let things pile up because we figure we will get organized once things "settle down."

3. No Organization = Put Items Anywhere & Everywhere

One of the quickest ways for your home to become disorganized is you simply don't know where things should go. And when you don't know what to do with it, you set it down anywhere. Then within a short period of time, you have an unruly disaster on your hands.

4. **Analysis Paralysis = Do Nothing Until Something Perfect Comes Along**
How could a perfectionist have clutter? While it is clear that you have clutter problem, you may not feel equipped to deal with it perfectly, so you do nothing instead. Maybe you don't have the perfect organization system; you don't feel like you have the proper amount of time to clean out the entire closet, or can't decide what is most important to do first.

Step 3: Clutter Is Ruining Your Life

Clutter isn't just a housekeeping issue; it's a health issue. Physical clutter creates emotional clutter, because the stress effects every aspect of your life. Every time you walk into your home, that clutter brings you down and reminds you of additional work that needs tending to. There's always a lingering sense of not feeling comfortable and emotionally free in your own living space.

While clutter has the power to cause depression and anxiety, it's doing a host of other things to your brain and your body.

BRAIN FOG

Clutter limits your brain's ability to process information, and can make you feel distracted. Clutter competes for your attention and wears down your ability to focus on other more important tasks.

SPIKES STRESS RELATED ILLNESSES

Your cortisol levels dramatically rise when coming home to a cluttered living space, but drops when you leave. Clutter overloads your senses, just like multitasking overloads your brain, causing you to be stressed and anxious.

CLUTTER INCREASES PROCRASTINATION

Clutter causes you so much stress that it begins making you feel overworked and tired. This leads to procrastination at home and at work. You are subconsciously burdened by the clutter and lack of organization.

CAN'T FIND ANYTHING

A cluttered home steals your valuable time. Think of the time you have spent just this week looking for papers, files, keys, cooking spices, purse, mis-matching socks, special pair of pants, marker, backpack, homework assignments and so on. We collectively waste 9 million hours per day searching for misplaced items, and nearly a quarter of us of admit to paying late penalties because we've lost bills.

PROVOKES ALLERGIES

Clutter makes it extremely difficult to really clean your environment. Thus, creating a germ haven that aggravates allergies of all kinds. Things that collect dust also collect dust mites, pet dander, and other household toxins.

STRESS HORMONES = WEIGHT GAIN

It is no secret, that an increase in stress hormones causes weight gain. However, it also contributes to bad habits that can translate in to over eating and the feeling of tiredness.

CLINGING TO THE PAST

Clutter is a way of clinging to the past. It is so overwhelming that it makes it harder for people to move forward in a positive way. The more overwhelmed we become, the less likely we will apply extra energy towards the attainment of future goals.

DRAINING THE LIFE OUT OF US

Over time, being surrounded by clutter slows us down, makes us feel mentally and physically fatigued. If we have a cluttered, disorganized living space, letting go of the stresses at work, finances, and our relationships, can be virtually impossible. if a workplace is in disarray, it can be difficult to complete tasks well and on time. Just sitting in a cluttered room can create stress, as it's a visual reminder of unfinished work.

The constant, low-grade stress can subtly and steadily drain our energy, leaving us overwhelmed, exhausted, and ultimately, physically ill. We know that long-term stress contributes to many chronic illnesses.

COMMON CONDITIONS
AGGRAVATED BY CHRONIC STRESS

EMOTIONAL SYMPTOMS OF STRESS INCLUDE:
➢ Becoming easily agitated, frustrated and moody.

> Feeling overwhelmed, like you are losing control or need to take control.
> Having difficulty relaxing and quieting your mind.
> Feeling bad about yourself, lonely, worthless and depressed.
> Avoiding others.

PHYSICAL SYMPTOMS OF STRESS INCLUDE:

> Low energy.
> Headaches.
> Upset stomach, including diarrhea, constipation and nausea.
> Aches, pains, and tense muscles.
> Chest pain and rapid heartbeat.
> Insomnia.
> Frequent colds and infections.
> Loss of sexual desire and/or ability.
> Nervousness and shaking, ringing in the ear.
> Cold or sweaty hands and feet.
> Excess sweating.
> Dry mouth and difficulty swallowing.
> Clenched jaw and grinding teeth.

In addition, the clutter that populates your home can encourage mold growth, bacteria, and other toxins. These pathogens can cause inflammation, respiratory conditions, and toxin buildup, leading to chronic illness down the road.

Step 4: Decluttering Boost Your Health & Vitality

Spring and fall seasons are the best times for releasing and letting go on all levels. In the spring, we can detoxify our environments, preparing for the abundance of new growth that comes with this warm season.

The release of excess clutter, allows us to create spaciousness, energy, and inspiration on all levels. In the fall time, we can benefit greatly by reorganizing and properly storing away warm weather items, and begin preparing for the winter. This is a process that our bodies understand naturally.

FREE YOURSELF

Organization of our external environment leads to clarity, efficiency, and less energy consumption. With a properly decluttered and organized home, all aspects of life are less congested and health flows more smoothly. Once people declutter and become better organized, many report the "letting go" process gave them a sense of lightheartedness and freedom. A simplified and organized life, allows you to realize what is truly important to you. By eliminating the physical junk around you, you are able to focus on the bigger picture, spend more quality time with the positive people in your life, and accomplish the goals you couldn't have otherwise.

Step 5: Dangers of A Messy Desk at Work

Is your monitor framed with layers of sticky-notes? Is your desktop hidden under stacks of papers, or your client's chairs buried under a pile of outerwear?

With so many open office plans today, more people can see into your workspace, and they do judge. Clutter undermines your productivity and motivation. 97% of employers firmly believe that your performance coincides with your workspace cleanliness and organization. When it's organized and precise, you have the mindset and motivation to work.

If you have let your clutter get out of control, you may not be sending your boss the message you intended.

WHAT YOUR BOSS THINKS WHEN YOU HAVE A MESSY DESK:
1.   Clients will think we are not qualified to handle their business.

2. I don't know if the employee is being productive?
3. I don't have confidence in their ability to organize company paperwork properly.
4. I am afraid that they are losing important documents.
5. Theft occurs when someone doesn't care about their job.
6. If they cannot properly manage themselves, they cannot oversee others.
7. Are they really qualified for the job?
8. Is their personally life affecting them at work?
9. I am worried things are not getting done correctly.
10. They appear to be wasteful with time and office supplies.

Step 6: Life Is Out of Control

There are screaming kids, crazy pets, racing to work, racing to school, the laundry is overflowing, and you had to dig through the dirty hamper to find your sons baseball uniform that should have been washed. Stress chemicals are running rampant, and irritability and panic set in as well as resentment of the household, job, family and everything else.

Does your automobile look like a homeless person's shopping cart? If so, none of your major environments are peaceful. There is nothing pleasant about your surroundings, and this is a major problem that needs to be solved now.

Many people blame the fact they work full-time, or that having kids makes decluttering/organizing and storing impossible. Well, none of this is true. It is easier to keep a busy family organized, then it is to continue living in an environment that is full of things you don't need, in places they shouldn't be. This waste your time, money, and most of all cost you your sanity.

Running around out of control, being chronically late, never being able to find things, and having a dirty or sloppy house are stressful conditions. Look around your house. It should be your perfect sanctuary, not a torture chamber screaming your name to come clean it.

Step 7: Clutter = Wasted Money

When your home is in a complete disarray, and you know you had something laying around somewhere but you can't seem to find it, so you go to the store and purchase another. This is one of the most common places people waste their hard-earned money. Because of their clutter and lack of organization, they continue to buy things in which they do not need or already have.

COMMON ITEMS REPURCHASED BY ACCIDENT

- ✓ Erasers we didn't know we had, so we bought a new package- **Wasted Money.**
- ✓ Can of sauce hidden in the back of the pantry, purchased new one – **Wasted Money.**
- ✓ Bathroom cleaner in the wrong place, so you picked up a new bottle – **Wasted Money.**
- ✓ Black shirt stuffed in the back of closet, replaced for special occasion – **Wasted Money.**

- ✓ Office supplies strung in every drawer, restocked for school – **Wasted Money.**
- ✓ Tools lost in the messy garage, had to pick up another for a project – **Wasted Money.**
- ✓ Dozens of socks with no match, replaced so we could wear our shoes – **Wasted Money.**
- ✓ Sporting equipment disappears, had to repurchase for practice – **Wasted Money.**

Save thousands of dollars each year buy properly organizing and storing household items. This way, when you need an item, it is easily located, used and put back for next time.

Step 8: Storage Methods Will Not Solve Problems Alone

While we might feel like the solution is to get containers to organize it all, it really makes more sense to do the obvious, eliminate the excess first. You really can't and should not attempt to organize an excess of clutter. If you are emotionally attached to things you don't have room for, look for creative ways to preserve memories without keeping every single item.

Storing your clutter into special containers will not declutter your home. It will not solve your anxiety, it will not prevent messy behavior. In fact, when organizing a mass amount of useless junk with important items, you are just making matter worse. The house or garage will soon return to its former state, and you will be back to square one.

Do not bother with organization until you have begun decluttering first.

Step 9: Divide & Decide Decluttering Method

The process of decluttering seems rather simple. However, when faced with the task of having to classify your belonging, things start to get a little more complicated. But if you really desire to remove stress, stop wasting money and time, and have a home that people admire, you must take this process very serious.

THERE ARE ONLY TWO QUESTIONS THAT YOU WILL HAVE TO ASK YOURSELF

1. Do I get rid of it?
2. Or, keep it and find a practical place to organize and store it?

We will be using the help of 2 storage bins clearly labeled **"Get Rid Of"** and the other **"Keep."**

Step 10: Organize Entire Home by Category – Not by Room

When we begin the process of decluttering, our initial urge is to organize and categorize items by individual rooms. However, our home is full of similar items in different rooms across our entire living space.

The key to proper organization is to find one practical place to store each item, regardless of what other room we find one in. The only exception to this rule is the bathrooms. You probably don't want to run to another room to grab your toothbrush, comb and shampoo.

COMMON ITEMS THAT WE FIND SCATTERED ACROSS MANY ROOMS

> ➤ Scissor can be found in bathrooms, kitchen, home office, laundry room, bedrooms and craft areas.
> ➤ Books can found in studies, home office, living room, family room, bedrooms, and on book shelves.

➢ Lotion can be found by the sinks, bathrooms and bedrooms.
➢ Things like: chap-stick, pens, flashlights, phone/computer chargers, nail polish, clippers, notebooks, paper clips, batteries, and controllers can be in several rooms throughout the house.

Step 11: Setting Up Practical Organization & Storage

Think carefully before you start putting together a plan of organization. Where you choose to store your items will either be great and practical, or inconvenient and annoying. If you begin organizing and storing items in one place, then realize it would work better in another, then relocate it.

Decluttering your home only works long-term if you make it easy for yourself to put things away in their correct places. If you normally use clippers in your bathroom, then storing all of them in your laundry room would be impractical. This inconvenient storage location would eventually cause you or a family member to begin leaving them laying around in the places they are most commonly used.

- **Store things sensibly.** Once you've finished purging unnecessary items, organize and store them in a logical place based on what they're used for, and how often you need them. This way, the whole family knows where to look for things and where to put them back.

- **Build organization into your daily routine.** No matter how you have organized, your home will need periodical reevaluation. As schedules shift, habits change, and families grow, organization that once worked flawlessly may need updated.

Stop and take notice when you find yourself or members of the household creating clutter piles. Why are you setting things there, instead of putting them away? Maybe your bills pile up on the coffee table because you don't have a bill paying or recycling system. Maybe your kids toss coats and homework on the kitchen table because they don't have designated hooks or routines to deal with things they bring home from school.

Once you can identify why the problem is occurring, make time to set up a new way to organize based on their piling habits.

Step 12: Declutter Organize & Store All at Once

To really declutter, organize and store your entire home properly, you will need to do it with speed. For some, completing the process may take days, while others will take months. This will depend on how packed your home is, how fast you can "Divide and Decide;" along with the amount of time you can donate to organizing and storing the kept items.

WHERE TO START FIRST

When beginning this process is easier to start by choosing a room, or area, that is not heavily used. When you have selected your first space, it's time to place your two bins beside you, and begin the "Divide and Decide" decluttering method.

Each item you pull out of a drawer, closet or off the floor, you must ask yourself the same two questions:

1. Do I get rid of it?
2. Or, to keep it and find a practical place to organize and store it?

Do I want to get rid of this item?
Before tossing it in the "Get Rid Of" bin, think about it. Does the item have a purpose? Will you use this item now or in the future? If you get rid of it, will you just need to buy it again at a later date?

If you can't find a good reason to keep it, then go ahead and toss it out.

Step 13: Refrain & Contain

If I could give you three tips, for maintaining a clean, simple, organized home, it would be these:

1. Get rid of as much stuff as you can.
2. Organize your home using practicality and convenience.
3. And quit buying stuff you don't absolutely need.

This might sound obvious and over simplistic, but it's true. It's impossible to keep a clean home when you're buried in stuff. If you really want a simpler, easier-to-manage household, you have to start with a major purge.

Once you have decluttered, you need to organize your remaining items using common sense and what is the most convenient. Lastly, you need to refrain from buying more, and contain the items properly using your new organizational system.

HOLIDAY GIFTS

If the idea of asking people to curb their gift-giving is disturbing, then it's even more vital to exercise restraint yourself. Otherwise all your effort will parish and you will find yourself right back at square one.

Step 14: Raise A Clutter Free Child

Kids today have far more than they need. If you take the time to go through their things together, you will be surprised at what they're willing to let go of. Start by helping them identify what's special, important, and useful. Then it will be much easier for your children to take responsibility and care for their remaining items.

Help your children organize regularly because they're calmer and more content in an orderly environment. Look how happy they are in their nice, clean room. They want to spend time there.

Organization is an important life skill that children need to learn in order to become successful adults. Which is why teaching them that "stuff" doesn't equal more happiness, but it can equate to a messy unproductive existence. Stress the importance of organization, responsibility, taking care of their things, and being a good steward of resources. Just as you teach them the importance of politeness, being kind, or doing their homework on time. Children look to you, as parents, to help them organize their environment, because they're often unable to do it for themselves.

HERE ARE SOME TIPS

1. **Quit buying them tons of stuff.** Kids today just have too much, far more than they're capable of taking care of. Instead give them a unique experience or a

lasting memory. This could include bringing them to the zoo, or setting up a slip-n-slide party in the back yard.

2. **Insist on order.** Children need to learn from an early age that part of their responsibility as members of the family is to care for their home, and the things they use. It's not fair to the rest of the family if kids are allowed to destroy the house. Make your expectations very clear, and establish consequences when they're not met.

3. **Teach the importance of charity.** Each year donate unwanted clutter to your local charity to be used for the better good of the community.

4. **Make picking up and putting away easy for them.** Make sure that bins are easy to reach, and to open. Create designated places for each of their belongings. If you

want organized kids, you have to give them the proper kid friendly setup.

5. **Acknowledge your space limits**. Teach your children that you can't have more books than will fit on your bookshelf, or more clothes than will fit in your closet. Be a good example for your kids by keeping your own space in order, because they learn the most from what they see you doing.

6. **Make organizing a regular part of your routine.** Your entire family will enjoy this process because they know how good they feel when it's done. Make sure that when you bring home a new item, the proper place to store it is determined immediately.

7. **Take a picture.** If your children are having trouble letting go of a something, take a picture of it, and write about your memories in their scrapbook. This makes the letting-go process much easier.

8. **Trial separation.** If your kids have an item that they just can't decide on, try putting it away for a trial period, such as a month. If they don't ask to play with it during that time, you can feel free to let it go. Make sure that you are honest about what you are doing, and the length of time they have.

9. **Praise and reward them for their efforts**. When you finish decluttering, and organizing, tell them how proud you are that they made good decisions.

Step 15: Kitchen Cleanse

Kitchens are one of the easiest rooms in the home to declutter, organize and store. The items here are less emotional than in many of the other rooms. The best way to tackle a kitchen is by selecting one area of concern first, like pots and pans or cups and plates. Empty the cabinets and cupboards into the middle of the floor and begin the "Divide and Decide" decluttering method. Fill one bin with the items you want to get rid, and the other of things you want to keep.

Once this is complete, wipe the area clean before organizing the keep pile into its proper place of storage.

FOLLOW THE SIMPLE STEPS

- Create a clean space for sorting.
- If you can't remember the last time it was used, sayonara.
- Get rid of the random dishes that don't belong to a set.
- Toss coffee stained, chipped mugs.

- Limit the number of reusable water bottles.
- Separate utensils used for cooking on the stove and gadgets into two drawers.
- Put in drawer dividers.
- Streamline kids dishes and cups. Throw away pieces that have seen better days.
- Stop buying random sippy cups, instead buy sets so they all fit together.
- Add a basket for kid lids, straws, and pieces.
- Toss the mismatched and stained containers. Then invest is smaller glass sets that stack.
- Add a basket for container lids
- Put in baskets and labels for food in pantry.
- Throw out old spices.
- Start only buying the food you need for one week, so the fridge stays organized and you don't waste food.

- Put a small basket on the counter for those little things that are always sitting around.
- If there is still not enough space for everything, it means more must go.

Step 16: Guide to Tackling the Spice Cabinet

Keeping your spices organized and fresh matters. It may not automatically make you the ultimate chef, but it will make you more effective at preparing a yummy family dinner. An organized spice rack means spices that you can actually find to use. Along with spices that are not past their expiration date.

TAKE A MOMENT TO ASK YOURSELF THIS QUESTION:

Which spices are cooked with regularly?
- Which spices do you need for everyday cooking and which one are just used on occasion? You're not doing yourself any favors by holding on to spices you never use.
- Start The Purge.....

STUFF YOU DON'T RECOGNIZE

If you have no clue what these things are or how they got into your kitchen, you should throw them away.

STUFF YOU RECOGNIZE BUT DON'T USE OFTEN

If you see a spice and can't immediately think of two or three delicious things you want to cook with it, throw it away. You can always get more down the road when needed.

THE KEEPERS:

These are your everyday spices. You know what they are and you use them often. But are they fresh, or is it time for an upgrade? Spices don't really go bad, per se, but in general, older spices become stale tasting.

Step 17: Junk-Drawer Perfection In 30 Minutes

You may call it your "catch all," or your "multi-use drawer" but let's be honest, it's a really a junk drawer.

This is the place you store all the items you either rarely use, or don't know where else it should go. But even junk drawers can be neat and tidy with a little decluttering and some simple organization tips.

The goal of a junk drawer is to provide a place to store all of those little odds and ends that don't quite fit in anywhere else. In your kitchen, this might be your scissors, rubber bands, twist ties and a notepad and pens. None of those items belong in the utensil drawer or the spice cabinet, but they are used frequently and need to be stored out of sight in a convenient location.

DECLUTTER THE JUNK DRAWER

Take everything out and then Divide and Decide. Use your two bins to sort out what you want to get rid of and the items you want to keep. Do you really need a stockpile of soy sauce packets, or lids from pens you can't find? Should you keep old business cards from years ago. Of course not! Keep what really matters and get rid of the rest.

Once your drawer is empty, take the opportunity to wipe it out. This will reduce dust mites, household toxins, mold and sticky liquids that may have leaked.

GET STARTED

Sort, group, and arrange into piles. You will find some items that don't belong in the junk drawer. Put those aside and continue to stack the remaining content. The beauty of the junk drawer is that everyone has their own unique junk, but there are a few essentials items that can make your junk drawer more user-friendly.

JUNK DRAWER ESSENTIALS

- Kitchen Junk Drawer
- Coupon holder
- Recipe sorter
- Pens and pencils
- Scissors
- Office Junk Drawer:
- Label maker
- Stapler, scissors, tape dispenser
- Headache medicine, band aids, antibacterial ointment
- Loose change
- Hand sanitizer

➤ **Plan storage solutions.** Measure the width and height of your drawer and decide which hardware you will use to divide your items. It's a great idea to use small trays in varying sizes.

CREATIVE AND UNEXPECTED JUNK DRAWER DIVIDERS

- The expand-a-drawer organizer
- 4-section drawer organizer
- Shallow drawer organizers

- Deep drawer organizers
- Muffin tins
- Ice cube trays
- Makeup trays

Arrange your storage. Arrange the items in their new dividers. Even if the contents of your drawer remain a mishmash. The key to an organized drawer is to be able to see what's in there quickly, rather than digging through it making a worse mess then before.

Maintain junk drawer organization. Go through your junk drawer on a regular basis. Upkeep is crucial.

Step 18: Bathroom Solutions

Decluttering and organizing a bathroom can have its challenges. The space is normally limited and the stuff is normally out of control. The bathroom is an important room in the house because its stores everything from shampoo, razors, towels, combs, hair bands, lotions, tooth brush, nail polish, clippers, to first aid supplies. Since many of the items are small, it makes decluttering more time consuming. In addition, the bathroom is a high traffic area that has to be organized conveniently, so it feels right to put things back in their correct place.

Start by taking everything out of your bathroom and putting them in a dedicated area. Have your two bins ready so that you can Divide and Decide what things you will get rid of, and things you want to.

SOLUTIONS TO BATHROOM STORAGE NEEDS

SEE THROUGH
See-through containers are essential when you need to grab and go. Stock your shelves with a mix of acrylic, plastic, and glass holders that show off supplies.

ROLL OUT
Space under a sink is one of your bathroom's most spacious storage. Try using a two-tier pullout shelf, or narrow top shelf that glides past the plumbing. Adhesive, undercabinet lighting makes every corner visible.

REMOVE DRAWER FRONTS
A vanity style cabinet with open shelves allows easy access to toiletries. Use the shelving to showcase baskets and trays.

STICK WITH IT
Maximize space by hanging a magnetic knife strip and adhesive containers. Stick metal nail tools and bobby pins on the strip.

PARTY DIP
Use a party dip try to keep lip balm, lotion, and other nightly essentials organized.

SWIVEL STORAGE
Easy access is essential in hard-to-reach bathroom cabinets. Make use of a spinning turntable to organize glass jars filled with disposable items. Use labels from a vinyl decal sheet and accent with adhesive letters or scrapbook stickers.

TUCK AWAY TRASH
Keep a trash-can out sight by attaching it to a cabinet door.

SLIDE SIDEWAYS
Make your bathroom mirror work a little harder with space-saving drawers that pull out sideways.

BANK ON BASKETS

For bath supplies and towels, try using decorative baskets. The containers help organize cabinets while concealing objects that you don't wish to display. Simple labels made with paper tags and string make it easy to identify contents.

NESTLE IN A NOOK

A floor-to-ceiling hutch-style cabinet makes it easy to load up a guest bath for hosting. Fill the open shelves with items for each guest, including towels and toiletries. Contain cleaning supplies in a closed lower cabinet.

ON-THE-WALL

Wall-hung containers that are dishwasher-safe, such as this kitchen utensils holder, can make a great toothbrush holder. This leaves your sink area clean and more spacious.

BUMPED-IN STORAGE CABINET

Extra space between the bathroom wall studs, can provide easy storage. Even if the space between rooms is shallow, shelves built floor-to-ceiling between studs can hold a large amount of supplies and toiletries.

REPURPOSED STORAGE

A small ladder beside the toilet offers a spot to rest hand towels, reading materials, and adds decorative elements. With a fresh coat of paint, the old ladder is transformed.

FLOATING SHELF

Try using a floating shelf below a pedestal sink. The shelf provides easy-access towel storage. It could also be used for toiletries or small storage bins.

TOWEL HANGERS

Towel and robe hooks are great for holding extra towels that are handy to use. You can find "his" and "her" hooks that give a unique feel.

PLAYTIME STORAGE

A mobile storage caddy provides a convenient spot to place toys, washcloths, and other bath-time essentials. When bath time is over, simply allow the items in the caddy to drip-dry over the tub. Also, a hanging fruit basket for children's bathroom toys can work well.

SEATED STORAGE

A cushioned bench with a wide drawer at its base, can store extra towels and bathing necessities within arm's reach of the shower.

Step 19: Transform Your Closet

There's no point in buying the latest bag or dress, if you can't find it in your closet when you're getting dressed. A clutter free, well-organized wardrobe means you'll maximize all your purchases, and come out looking polished even on hectic mornings.

The task of de-cluttering your wardrobe can be overwhelming, so Divide and Decide carefully, then be sure to exercise Refrain and Contain thereafter.

SMART WAYS TO MAXIMIZE SPACE AND PROPERLY ORGANIZE

1. Pegboard mounted inside a closet door creates an inexpensive mini-dressing station.
2. Pool noodles keep boots upright and breathing.
3. Stack T-shirts upright if using a drawer. Now you can see which shirts are there.
4. Tie knot all your scarves around a hanger.

5. Use satin hangers for more delicate items and sturdy wood hangers for tailored jackets.
6. Organize nail polish by color using shoe organizer.
7. Get a hanging laundry hamper.
8. Hang your shorts/pants with shower rings instead of hangers.
9. Use pillow cases to keep matching sheet sets together.
10. Holiday ornament boxes make great sock organizers.
11. Hang suitcases over the door.
12. Double hanger space by using tabs from soda cans.
13. Forget expensive jewelry organizers just use ice cube trays.
14. Organize and charge gadgets within night stand drawer.
15. Store out of season clothes in comforter bags.

Step 20: Store Your Beauty Products, Beautifully!

Say goodbye to your messy makeup drawer and medicine cabinet! These solutions will help you clear clutter so you'll never lose another eyeshadow or nail polish again.

GLAM UP YOUR BATHROOM

1. Display pretty fragrances on top of a cake stand.
2. Arrange your everyday beauty products on a revolving spice rack to save space.
3. Store liner pencils, mascara, or brushes in a glass jar.
4. Fill a flower vase with coffee beans or beads, and stick your brushes inside for easy access.
5. Separate your products by category inside of a kitchen utensil tray to organize your makeup drawer.
6. Store your hot tools inside of a decorative magazine holder.
7. Hang your hot tools on adhesive hooks inside of a cabinet door.

8.   Use the pouches on a hanging shoe organizer to store larger hair products.
9.   Save space by stacking hairspray bottles on a wine-rack.
10. Use a desk file organizer to display and store makeup palettes.
11. Stick your eyeshadow singles into ice tray slots, so you can see all the shades at once.
12. Use a jewelry organizer to visibly store small makeup products.
13. Adhere magnets to the back of your makeup compacts, and stick them on a metal board to save space and decorate your walls.
14. Arrange your makeup in clear desk organizers.
15. Line your drawers with glass food containers to neatly organize cotton balls, sponges, and other makeup application tools.
16. Stick cotton swabs inside an old candle vase.
17. Store your nail polishes in a cute cookie jar.

18. Stack lip glosses and lipsticks on the tiers of a cupcake tray.
19. Use a mini loaf pan to neatly organize your lip shades or other small products inside a drawer.
20. Stack your hair ties on a decorative wine bottle.

Step 21: Organizing Pet Supplies

When you need your pet's brush, do you end up spending an hour looking around the entire house? When you find the brush, it was under the bed or became a chew toy? Organizing pet supplies doesn't have to be a complicated endeavor.

If you have dozens of old torn toys laying around, or leashes that have seen better days, just keep one or two in reserve and toss the rest out. Then, you can find containers that are suitable for the space.

FUN WAYS TO ORGANIZE PET SUPPLIES

1. **Create a take a walk station by the door.** Storing dog leashes can be a pain, they tend to dominate most drawers. Strategically, near the door is the best location for leashes, harnesses and other walking related items. Hang a tote bag on a hook at the front door, or a nearby closet.

2. **Put all pet toys in one place.** If you have had for a pet for any length of time, you know that the number of toys can adds up quickly. A good thing to do is to collect all the toys and put them in one large and convenient storage container. A cute option for dog toys is a bone shaped storage bin or a large bone shaped basket.

3. **Dedicate a shelf, cabinet or drawer for your pet's needs.** Pets, like other family members require everyday items, which can quickly become clutter if you don't keep it under control. If you have a hutch, cabinet, spare drawer or shelf, dedicate the empty space for your pets.

4. **Keep pet grooming supplies in a portable caddy.** Portable caddies are perfect for organizing all your pet's grooming supplies. You can take it out when its bath time, and store it quickly when done. Its handy and makes bath time a little easier.

5. **Create a pet treat station.** An old cookie jar or even a fancy new one would be perfect for organizing your pet's treats. Add some decorative labels and you have yourself a beautiful treat station.

6. **Create a better way to store pet food.** Storing dry food in an airtight stackable bin, made especially for that purpose, helps saves on space and keeps food fresh.

7. **Create a feeding station away from traffic.** Food and water bowls are always in everyone's way. They are kitchen obstacles, easy to knock over and kick across the floor. Consider an organized feeding station to minimize clutter.

8. **Keep pet records organized in one folder.** Keeping your pet's vital documents in an easily accessible place can sometimes be a matter of life or death. Create a file for each pet containing all pertinent information, such as food, medications, and allergens. If

you need to leave your pet with others, everything they need to know is in this one folder.

Organizing pet supplies requires cooperation of everyone who lives there. But if you take the time to purge and organize, not only will you enjoy the ease of finding things, but your pet will also be happy they have their own special place.

Remember to:
> Divide and Decide.
> Create clearly defined areas for specific pet items like toys, grooming supplies and food in convenient locations.
> Categorize similar things together in one designated place.
> Find a way to store things in a pretty way - either hide the items behind cabinets or concealed in storage containers or baskets.

➢ once you have organized, put things back in its designated place every day to keep things under control.

Step 22: Decluttering Digital & Printed Pictures

People are very sentimental about family photos! They represent special memories, experiences, people, and feelings. It's our past and they are hard to part with.

DECLUTTERING DIGITAL PHOTOS:

- ❖ Delete duplicate photos. Keep the 1 or 2 great ones and declutter the rest.

- ❖ Delete blurry photos.

- ❖ Delete pictures that just had a temporary purpose (pics you took of items when you were shopping so you could refer to them later or show someone else).

- ❖ Remember, even though these pictures are digital and don't take up a lot of physical space in your home, they can become overwhelming.

decluttering printed photos

❖ First, decide what your goal is for your printed photos. How do you want to enjoy your photos? In albums, scrapbooks, boxes, frames, etc.?

❖ Consider how they will be stored and how you will protect them from being damaged. Or maybe you want to declutter and scan to digital copies.

❖ Now go through your photos and get rid of the images that don't have special meaning. They could be of people who don't remember, people you don't want to remember, places you don't recall, etc.

❖ If you have old photos and you would like to know the history, you can either try to find out from other family members. If you are not interested in knowing, you can see if other family members would like the photos you're letting go of.

❖ Just as with other sentimental items,
search for the treasures and let go of the
rest. You will appreciate being able to flip
through a few special albums and
sharing stories.

Step 23: Garage Overhaul

If you're like most of the world, your car is a five-figure investment that you can't live without. Why leave it outdoors, where it can suffer damage from UV exposure, bird droppings, tree sap and flying basketballs from the neighborhood kids? In addition, leaving your car outside in the summer means climbing into a scalding-hot vehicle.

Then when it turns winter, your will have the privilege of sitting on freezing cold seats after you have spent 20 minutes scaping the snow off all windows. Storing your car in a garage will keep it a lot cleaner, prolong its life and your own.

THE BIG CLEAN-OUT

Did you know that over 70 percent of car owners can't park inside their own garage. The reason? Too much stuff and not enough room.

TAKE BACK THE GARAGE

- Set aside at least a full day, or even a full weekend.
- Make decluttering a family project, it will go a lot faster.
- Go through everything, including boxes you didn't unpack when you moved in. Who knows maybe you find some hidden treasure.
- Divide and Decide on the things to get rid of and those that you will keep.
- Sort the keepers into broad categories (for example, sports equipment, hand tools), and place them in well-marked cardboard boxes or, better yet, stackable clear-plastic bins you can use later. Put the keepers back in the garage for now.

- As soon as possible, donate giveaways and or schedule a yard sale to get rid of unwanted stuff.

THINGS YOU SHOULD NOT BE STORING IN YOUR GARAGE

- Paper Products – they attract rodents, mildew and mold.
- Freezer or additional refrigerator – uses a large amount of power in a warm garage.
- Propane tanks – sparks could ignite a tank filled with propane, keep this outdoors.
- Pet Food - Possums and other critters will sniff it out. Keep it in a sealed container inside.

GREAT STORAGE IDEAS FOR A WELL-ORGANIZED GARAGE

- Use a slat wall to hang and organize smaller accessories.
- Or try a pegboard wall one instead.
- Keep every tool in its proper place with outlines or labels on your pegboard or slat wall.

- Have a spare chest of drawers hanging around? Turn them into a workbench.
- Install a set of old school lockers and assign one to each member of your family.
- Create extra space and store bikes vertically or hang them from the ceiling.
- Or use a stack of vintage crates.
- Repurpose empty coffee cans as miniature recycling centers.
- Make your mudroom inside the garage, and not allowing the filth inside your home.
- Conserve space with a fold-up worktable.
- Put a pallet to work as sports equipment storage, by attaching the slats to the wall or pegboard.
- Keep sports balls contained with a wire basket hanger.
- Store spray-paint or auto cans in a shoe organizer.
- Don't leave bicycles and scooters toppled over in a corner--use a rack to safely park them.

- Or create designated parking spaces for your children's vehicles using tape.
- Hang up a magnetic strip to hold screwdrivers, wrenches, and scissors.
- Utilize the space above your garage door with mounted shelving.
- Painting on a concrete floor makes it easier to clean and helps protects your garage from mildew.
- Use large metal buckets to store children's outdoor toys.
- Consolidate leftover paint into jars and properly label.

Final Thoughts

The benefits of minimalism stretches far beyond minimizing the visual clutter. Decluttering your space can lead to both physical and mental freedom. Emotional stress can be reduced, clarity, focus, and concentration improved, guilt and anxiety melts away.

When our home is a space we feel comfortable and content in, our mental wellbeing will dramatically improve. Being mindful of our environment boost our happiness levels. You will feel more creative and productive than ever before.

Reducing your material possessions leaves your living space in a simplistic state. You'll find your home stays cleaner for longer, and you'll do to less housework to maintain it. After seeing the amount of stuff you have accumulated over the years, and subsequently had to get rid of; the costs of those unwanted items is painful. These items serve as a reminder for us to be conscious consumers and to only buy things we truly need.

www.ingramcontent.com/pod-product-compliance
Lightning Source LLC
Chambersburg PA
CBHW060140050426
42448CB00010B/2219